GHOSTLY
ENCOUNTERS

Peter Underwood

BOSSINEY BOOKS

ACKNOWLEDGMENTS

The author gratefully acknowledges the help he has received in preparing this volume and the permissions to quote from, among others, Donald Armstrong, MBE, Garry Bissell, Mrs Marianne Burge, David Crawford, Lisa Crawford, Miss C. Curthoys, Miss Catherine Edwards, Lorraine Fisher, Michael Goss, Mrs Patricia A. Hall, Martin Kelsey, Win and Harry Kilbey, Margery and Barry Knowles, Roger Little, Jamie Owen, Jon Pertwee, Mrs C. Piper, Chief Inspector J. Sait, Alexandra Scull, George Smith, E.T. Smith, Paul Soulsby, Miss N.A. Thorn; also the Exeter *Express and Echo* and other local newspapers and periodicals.

Front cover design: MAGGIE GINGER
Front cover photography: RAY BISHOP
Back cover photography: RAY BISHOP
Drawings: FELICITY YOUNG

First published in 1992 by Bossiney Books, St. Teath, Bodmin, Cornwall.

Typeset and printed by Penwell Ltd., Callington, Cornwall

ISBN 0 948158 74 3

*For my wife Joyce
with much love and
eternal gratitude for
sharing with me several
ghostly encounters*

About the author – and the book

PETER UNDERWOOD *has been President of the Ghost Club (founded 1862) since 1960 and has probably heard more first-hand ghost stories than any man alive. A long-standing member of The Society for Psychical Research, Vice-President of the Unitarian Society for Psychical Studies, a member of the The Folklore Society, The Dracula Society and a former member of the Research Committee of the Psychic Research Organisation, he has lectured, written and broadcast extensively. In 1987 he was elected a Fellow of the Royal Society of Arts.*

He took part in the first official investigation into a haunting; has sat with physical and mental mediums, and conducted investigations at seances, been present at exorcisms, experiments at dowsing, precognition, clairvoyance, hypnotism, regression; conducted world-wide tests in telepathy and extra-sensory perception, and has personally investigated scores of haunted houses.

In 1983 Peter Underwood made his debut for Bossiney with Ghosts of Cornwall. *His titles for Bossiney include* Westcountry Hauntings *and* Mysterious Places. *In this, his eighth title for the Cornish cottage publishers, he explores* Ghostly Encounters *in six areas: Cornwall, Devon, Somerset, Avon, Dorset and Wiltshire – many of his accounts appearing in print for the first time – and all Felicity Young's drawings have been especially commissioned for this publication.*

TO SEE A GHOST ...

IF YOU crave a ghostly encounter you could not do better than visit the Westcountry: Cornwall, Devon, Dorset, Somerset, Wiltshire and Avon – it is truly a magical part of Britain and my wife and I look forward to our visits, often twice a year or more, as I suppose befits a President of the Ghost Club and his lady!

This selection of true ghost stories includes encounters with full seemingly-solid apparitions and with glimpses of shadowy forms; even with sounds of something unseen – just as mystifying and puzzling and frightening to the people present: all represent ghostly encounters that defy explanation and remind us that occasionally, and perhaps especially in this mysterious, evocative and surprising area where the unexpected often happens, there are influences, forces and powers about which we know little and over which we have no control. If you happen to be in the right place at the right time you will experience something; you do not have to believe in such things, you do not have to be a certain type of person, you do not have to be of any particular age, sex, religion, race or belief – these happenings are reported by every kind and type of person from every part of the world – but especially from the Westcountry.

I quote, almost at random, from a letter sent to me by Mrs Patricia Hall of Bristol in August 1991: 'My husband and I, two years ago, together with my son and his wife, stayed with friends in Penzance. They had purchased a rambling house . . .' (*but perhaps I should not describe or locate the house exactly, P.U.*) 'My husband and I shared a twin-bedded room and in the middle of the night I awoke very suddenly, icy cold, with the distinct impression of someone sitting on the end of my bed. I felt a weight beside my feet and experienced a slight bouncing sensation, exactly as you would if

'If you happen to be in the right place at the right time ...'

someone had sat heavily down beside you. I became increasingly frightened and could feel the hairs stand up on the back of my neck but, regretfully, I did not have the courage to look . . .

'I managed to awaken my husband and together we looked and needless to say, we saw nothing; and he laughed at my foolishness, but I had very little sleep for the rest of our stay.

'It was only recently that I told my son about it and instead of making fun of me he said that on the numerous occasions when he had stayed there while on business in Cornwall, he had experienced the identical thing; but he had never said anything to his hosts for fear of offending them . . .'

One day at the Savage Club I talked with Jon Pertwee, the actor and comedian, perhaps best known for his television role as Doctor Who, about a ghostly encounter which he shared with his brothers in Devon when they were young.

The Pertwees had a country house in Devon and while it was being extended the boys stayed at a little workman's cottage nearby; actually two cottages knocked into one with two downstairs sitting-rooms and two bedrooms. When their father went out in the evenings he used to say, 'You boys will be all right?' and they'd say, 'Yes, of course, we're fine.' Jon was sleeping in one bedroom with his stepbrother and there was a door through into the other bedroom where Michael, later to become a playwright and author, slept.

There was no television in those days and the cottage did not possess a radio so after a few games of Mah Jong or draughts, the boys usually turned in soon after nine o'clock and they were always relieved when their father came back to the house later to see that they were all right. He used to let himself in, come up the stairs and quietly open the door and then walk through into the next room to see that Michael was all right; then he'd go back downstairs and out of the back door. All the children liked to know that he checked on their well-being; it made them feel loved and wanted.

Then one evening when their father was going out to dinner with friends some miles away, the boys thoughtfully said to him, 'There's no need to come back to the house tonight, Dad, we'll be perfectly all right.' Their father looked at them rather strangely. 'What are you talking about?' he asked. 'Why should I come back?'

'Well, you usually do,' they said. And he replied, 'But I've never, ever come back here again after I've left you boys alone.'

There was no explanation but equally there was no doubt that the three boys had heard someone – or some thing – clump up the stairs, pass through one room and go into the second; and then back down the stairs and out of the back door. All three boys heard the sounds simultaneously, quite clearly and there was no doubt in their minds at the time that it was their father, but in fact on no occasion at those times had he been anywhere near the house.

Jon Pertwee added, sensibly, that there was no electricity in the wilds of Devon in those days and it was pitch dark so none of the boys had actually *seen* anything odd when the 'presence' had visited them but they were all satisfied that they must have had a ghostly encounter in Devon in the early '30s, when the only artificial light was gaslight and oil lamps. Oddly enough, after their father had told them that he never returned at night to the cottage, they did not hear the ghostly footsteps again and soon afterwards they moved back to the house, with lasting memories of a ghostly visitation that had been accepted as normal at the time.

The Westcountry means many things to many people. Just about everyone who visits these mystical and magical regions comes away with memories that last a lifetime – and not infrequently with a personal ghostly encounter that widens the horizons of experience and leaves a lasting, vivid and often moving and poignant memory in the reaches of the mind.

Peter Underwood
Savage Club
1 Whitehall Place
London SW1A 2HD

The man in the tunnel
Bincombe, Dorset

IN AUGUST 1991 a newspaper in Bournemouth alerted me to the fact that British Rail believed it had a ghost in a tunnel between Dorchester and Weymouth. Apparently for several successive Friday evenings, in the middle of Bincombe Tunnel, train drivers saw what appeared to be a human figure ahead of the train on the line, and at the same time the drivers heard what sounded like a collision.

When the trains stopped there was no sign of any human form or anything on the line ahead to account for what the drivers had seen; nor was there any evidence of any collision or anything to account for the sounds the drivers had heard.

There were stories of a missing person having met his death in the tunnel some years before but nothing concrete could be found to account for the sights and sounds that had been witnessed, by different people on different occasions; all experienced and dependable British Rail drivers.

I suggested that extra staff or an investigative team might be included in the drivers' cab as independent witnesses on one or two future journeys at the appropriate times, but I was told – somewhat to my surprise – that it was difficult to find such volunteers! I did suggest one or two Ghost Club Members in the vicinity whom I knew would be happy to oblige but in the event they were not approached.

British Rail was quite open in this instance and seemed convinced that its drivers, 'reliable, dependable and experienced', had indeed had a ghostly encounter. Quietly and persistently enquiries and investigations are proceeding . . .

◀ *'What appeared to be a human figure ahead of the train ...'*

The one-eyed miller
Boscastle, Cornwall

IN 1991 my wife and I spent a week at Boscastle and while we were there we heard about a one-eyed man who was supposed to haunt the Old Mill next door to the Wellington Hotel where we were staying. We talked to the proprietors of the Old Mill, Margery and Barry Knowles – the building is now used as a Craft Centre – Win and Harry Kilbey, who used to run a cafe and disco there, and Roger Little, the local potter and a mine of information on Boscastle; we also talked to one or two other inhabitants who had knowledge of the ghost of the Old Mill.

Long referred to locally as 'that haunted place', the mill had once been worked by a one-eyed miller who died amid rumours of being a murderer and having hidden 'something' somewhere in the building.

Once, a girl occupying a flat in the old building awoke suddenly to find a dark figure bending over her, a man with one eye. When she screamed the figure vanished. Later she glimpsed the same figure in daylight when it disappeared into a solid wall in the basement of the building, where the old mill workings were once housed.

Win and Harry Kilbey, retired psychiatric nurses, both experienced odd happenings during their sojourn at the Old Mill. There was the night Harry heard footsteps and the sound of falling sand in the roof area; no reason was ever discovered for these and other strange sounds. One visitor said he had heard 'someone walking about all night . . .'

Win, very busy one mid-day during the August rush in the cafe, went down to the basement, needing something from the deep-

freeze stored there and she found, just for a split second, that the whole basement area had returned to what it had been years previously, a working mill! As she opened the door to the basement there was the mill working as it had worked in the busy days of the one-eyed miller; the next moment everything had returned to normal and Win began to think she must have imagined it – but she knew she hadn't and she told us she can still remember seeing all the old machinery working away.

From time to time the lights in the Old Mill would go on by themselves. Several times the police were called but there was no sign of an entry and nothing had been taken or disturbed but the lights in the dark, empty and locked building had been switched on by 'something' – the one-eyed miller perhaps?

Once Harry Kilbey spent some time fixing cotton across the stairs and doorways and taping light switches but it made no difference; a few hours later he was called out again and the police accompanied him as he unlocked and opened the doors of the Old Mill and there were the lights all blazing away and otherwise everything as he had left it, including the cotton and tapes.

Doors, one in particular, would open and close without human contact and once Win saw a figure appear through the wall in the basement. She told me she couldn't really describe it, it all happened so quickly but it could have been a man in a smock, like a miller . . . The self-opening door was 'fixed' several times and by different people but it made no difference. Although there was no wind and the door had been re-hung and the latch checked and re-checked, no sooner did one walk away than the door would slowly open or when left open for a moment, it would softly and quietly close. Someone or something was being secretive.

My brief research at Boscastle revealed that three separate people on different occasions had seen the one-eyed man in the haunted mill and none of them at that time had been aware that the building was supposed to be haunted or that a one-eyed miller had once occupied the premises. And still odd things happen from time to time at the Old Mill at Boscastle . . .

◀ *The author beside the haunted mill at Boscastle.*

The cat that came in from the cold
Bristol, Avon

A FEW years ago a young lady wrote to me from Winterbourne, Bristol saying: 'I walked into a shop in the middle of Bristol and purchased your book on *Ghosts of Somerset*. Having read the book I am so impressed that I thought I would write to you and tell you of my experience. I am nineteen years old.

'Three years ago a stray cat visited us during the exceptionally cold winter. It soon adopted us and we found out that it used to live just up the road from us in a cul-de-sac. The owners did not look after the animal very well and we learned that it was called 'Smokey'. The cat was soon living with us and she had a habit of going out at night and she would stay out all night and return early in the morning. In the daytime she slept. Each morning she would jump on to the hut roof outside and then on to the roof of the garage, finally landing on my windowsill. There she would sit until I opened the window to let her in. I always heard her jump up on to the windowsill and bang against the window.

'Unfortunately on the 5th May Smokey was killed on the main road outside our house. It was a cool and misty morning and my father was going off to work when he found her. She was a pretty cat, well marked, distinctive and she had a good temperament and we were all very sad.

'The point concerning this happening is that the very next morning, at about four o'clock, there was a "bump" at my window. I got out of bed and pulled back the curtain and found to my astonishment that Smokey was on the windowsill! She walked along the sill

'Smokey was on the windowsill ...'

Bristol on a winter morning: a city with a large ghostly population.

and jumped down, disappearing from my sight. I rushed out of my bedroom and opened the landing window, expecting to see her there. I called and called but she had disappeared into thin air. It was very strange because we all knew she was dead. I am convinced that Smokey came back from the dead to thank us for being kind to her. I may say I searched the garden with a torch at the time and later but there was no sign of any cat. By now my mother was awake and wondering what I was doing; she decided that I had imagined it all but I can still see Smokey, and I like to think she remembered us. To me it was definitely a ghostly encounter.'

* * * * *

The figure in the mist
Cannington, near Bridgwater, Somerset

I HAVE before me a letter from Garry Bissell who tells me that when he was thirteen years of age he boarded at Brymore School of Agriculture at Cannington and he goes on: 'It was part of our duties to look after the various animals and on one particular morning another boy and myself were on milking duty, which meant we had to get up early and fetch the cows in for milking.

'It was a cold, misty morning and at about 6.30 a.m. the cows were in a field next to two ponds. We drove them across the driveway which led up to the school. My friend was at the front and I followed them from behind. I happened to glance round and in the mist I saw a very tall figure in what appeared to be a black robe, seemingly floating towards me but I could see no face.

'I stood there totally dumbfounded and watched it get nearer and nearer until it was about fifty yards away when I got a terrible feeling of evil and foreboding; a strange wind seemed to blow all round me and the cattle started to move very quickly . . . I was very frightened and I ran as fast as I could past the cattle to my friend. He too had seen the figure and we both ran to the school.

'When we were both inside the milking parlour I asked my friend if he had seen what appeared to be a tall figure in a black robe but no face and he said "Yes". We agreed not to tell anyone else from the school through fear of being disbelieved and teased but all this is totally true and this I swear.

'I have no logical explanation for what we both saw but I am sure that no one tricked us. Later I found that the school is very old and over the years the property has been owned by various lords of the manor including John Pym who was, I believe, a Parliamentarian many years ago . . . I look forward to any possible explanation.'

The enquiries I made resulted in no plausible explanation although several people I talked to mentioned similar experiences in the same area. The why and wherefore has yet to be discovered but perhaps in the right atmospheric surroundings and in the presence of certain people this unidentified being might well reappear.

* * * * *

The ghost children
Charfield, Avon

CHARFIELD, a rambling place on a hillside in the extreme north of Avon where the county borders with Gloucestershire, is the scene of some singular ghostly encounters. The beautiful and quiet old church with its 14th century porch and marvellous outer door enshrines a tragic memory. In the churchyard there is a memorial to twelve victims of the Charfield railway disaster of 1928; a disaster that left behind several ghosts.

In the darkness before dawn on October 13 the night passenger and mail train shrieked its way across the foot of the Cotswolds, the passengers dozing fitfully as they waited for the train to slow down into Bristol, the end of the line, and only a matter of minutes away.

Unknown to anyone aboard the express, a shunting engine was

puffing its laborious way across the main line, dragging heavily-laden trucks behind it. Suddenly, amid the drizzle and fog of that early morning, a thunderous and sickening crash awakened the sleeping villagers of Charfield. Then came a nightmare of shrieking, screaming and crying as injured and dying passengers struggled for survival amid tons of splintering woodwork and twisted and broken metalwork. And then a third train ploughed into the derailed express.

Forty-one people were badly injured, fourteen already dead. As Dr Walsingham Ward carried out his grisly examinations, searchers came across the pathetic, charred and almost unrecognisable remains of two more victims; they were small and almost certainly children. During the subsequent inquest fifteen of the dead were identified and named, two were not: those last two bodies that had been found, one a boy of about eleven, the other a girl of perhaps seven.

The so-called Ghost Children of Charfield were never claimed; they were never reported missing; never identified. Six of the victims of the crash were buried in a grave in the old Charfield cemetery, nine others in a small plot together with the mysterious children, whose grave was inscribed 'Two Unknown'.

Conductor Harry Haines of Gloucester Station had gone through the express collecting and clipping tickets and he swore that he saw two children travelling alone in a compartment near the front of the train; one a boy of eleven or twelve, the other a girl of eight or nine. But still no one ever came forward to claim or identify the children. Someone must surely have seen them off on their journey and someone must have been expecting their arrival; it almost seemed as though they were not of this world. And as the days and weeks passed reports began to accumulate of the forms of two children, a boy and a girl, being seen in the vicinity of the crash . . .

Exactly a year after the crash, on October 13 1929 to be exact, a chauffeur-driven car pulled up at the gates of the old cemetery. A woman, dressed from head to foot in black and with a thick black veil covering her face, stepped out of the car. She carried a posy of flowers which she took into the cemetery and placed on the grave marked by a memorial erected by the old London, Midland and Scottish Railway, the memorial inscribed with ten names and the evocative words: 'Two Unknown'. The woman stood for a moment looking at the grave and then she turned and hurried away. The following year she repeated her homage.

Meanwhile the people of nearby Bristol were entertained by a sensational court case involving one of their most respected citizens, Chief Constable James F. Watson who, it seemed, had misused public funds by sending some of his officials on holidays as rewards for their conscientious work. Watson was suspended and eventually dismissed.

It was the same James Watson who, as part of his official duties, had played a big part in organising rescue work after the Charfield collision and who had been involved in attempts to identify the mysterious pair of children killed in the crash. At first that seemed the extent of his connection with the mystery but when it transpired that he had disappeared, ugly whispers began to spread throughout the neighbourhood and further abroad.

It was suggested that the man driving the car at the cemetery had been the ex-Chief Constable and that he and the mystery woman knew more than had been revealed about the unnamed children. There was no search for James F. Watson as such; after all he was a free man but his absence added fuel to the rumours that continued to spread. Then, a couple of months after Watson had been dismissed, his great friend, a Bristol solicitor of some eminence, Francis Hapgood, received a telegram out of the blue. It read: 'Meet me at Waterloo Bridge tomorrow midnight' and it was signed, 'J. Watson'. London was 120 miles away but Hapgood set out and met his old friend as he had been requested to do.

Apparently they shook hands, spoke briefly, shook hands again and parted. Two days later the body of James Watson was found in the pleasure gardens at Eastbourne. Nearby lay an open, cut-throat razor. The coroner recorded an 'open verdict' which seemed a little odd, to say the least, since it would appear to have been a clear case of suicide. Or were there doubts about the death? Francis Hapgood died soon afterwards and the mystery was never solved.

The lady in black was not seen again but from time to time, to this day, there are reports of the ghostly figures of two children, a boy and a girl, wandering hand in hand in the area where the frightful railway crash took place more than sixty years ago.

The boy in pyjamas
The Draynes Valley, Cornwall

IN MAY 1991 Mrs Marianne Burge of Polbathic near Torpoint wrote to me as follows: 'I have just finished reading your book, *Westcountry Hauntings* and felt I must write to you about an experience my husband had about six years ago.

'It was when we first moved to Cornwall and were living in a large house in the Draynes Valley, between St. Cleer and Jamaica Inn at Bolventor. The house was known as Lower Langdon.

'There were two very large rooms downstairs, one we used as a bedroom and the other as a sitting-room. Upstairs were the kitchen, bathroom and another bedroom occupied by my eldest son who was then thirteen years old.

'I was in the habit of getting up several times each night to visit the bathroom upstairs (my youngest son's birth being imminent at the time). Just before my return from one such visit, my husband was lying in bed waiting for me when all of a sudden a boy aged about fifteen, appearing to be quite solid, put his head around the bedroom door and looked straight at my husband. The boy was wearing rather old-fashioned pyjamas in a blue or mauve paisley pattern.

'My husband was puzzled rather than frightened and on my return a few seconds later said, "Was that Matthew who came in just now?". If it *had* been Matthew, I could not have failed to have seen him as there was a long hallway and a flight of stairs from the bathroom. I had in fact checked that Matthew was asleep before coming back downstairs. In any case Matthew did not wear pyjamas in bed, just tee-shirts and shorts. My husband remarked that there was complete silence throughout the appearance of the boy, who appeared obviously taller and older than our son, in any case.

'As a matter of fact, although I never saw anything in the house, the atmosphere was unpleasant and heavy and I never liked being there on my own at night.

'A school-friend of my son's came to stay for the night some time after this incident. We had said nothing about it to Matthew as we didn't want to make him nervous. The friend went up the staircase and stood at the landing window. He went very pale and just said, "I don't want to stay here". We had to get his parents to take him home although he never did say what he had felt or seen and we felt he didn't want to be asked.

'Finally, unrelated, but strange all the same, when I first told my brother-in-law that I was expecting our second son (who spent the first six months of his life at the house) he told me he had already dreamt the following things: That the child would be a boy, that he saw the numbers 0200 and 9.8 (which we took to be the child's birthweight), and that he would be born as the morning dew lay on the ground.

'The day my son was born, I woke up as the waters broke. I checked the time: it was exactly 2.00 a.m. My son was born at 9.08 a.m. and the nurse remarked how beautiful the morning was with the sun sparkling on the dewy grass!

'My husband has seen several other things since we moved to Cornwall, including an apparition on a building site where he was rebuilding an old house. The man was later recognised from his description, by several local residents, as a previous occupant of the house.

'Lower Langdon Farm is a large house built of granite stone block. I have only been able to discover a few facts about its past. One is a story of an elderly man who supposedly shot himself in the grounds outside; and another that in fairly recent times the house was used as a rehabilitation centre for alcoholics and tramps. No trace of a young boy has been found so far . . .'

In thanking Mrs Burge for her most interesting letter I asked whether the ghost boy withdrew from the doorway, disappeared where he was, or what? I also asked permission to reproduce the story in this book.

Mrs Marianne Burge was kind enough to say: '. . . we would be happy to have our ghost included in your new book and please feel free to include any information you require.' She added: 'I believe the property may have been re-sold recently as when we last travelled past, a few changes seemed to have taken place. It would be very satisfying if the account did jog someone's memory and provided us with an explanation as to the boy's identity.'

In reply to my enquiry Mrs Burge went on: 'You ask whether the ghost withdrew out of the room, or whether it simply disappeared. My husband states that it stared straight at him, then turned and he watched it leave the room. It must have "disappeared" before I returned a few seconds later (unless I did not "see" it – although I have been interested in ghost hunting myself for a number of years and have spent nights in haunted houses, etc; unfortunately I do not believe myself to be very sensitive to them). So it may be that only my husband, who I think is very sensitive, although very matter-of-fact about it, was the only one who could "see" the boy.'

I cannot help wondering who the boy could possibly have been . . . perhaps a former occupant; perhaps a visitor returning to somewhere he had been happy, or unhappy; perhaps the son of a former occupant who peeped into a room one day long ago and saw – what? Perhaps the son or grandson of the man who shot himself? It is all very intriguing and I would be most interested to hear from anyone who thinks they might be able to throw any light on the mystery boy of Lower Langdon.

* * * * *

'… mystical and magical regions …'

The persistent Miss Sarah
Falmouth, Cornwall

MISS Catherine Edwards of Falmouth wrote to me a year or two ago recounting in some detail the ghostly activity encountered there for a period extending over twenty years! I reproduce the account virtually as it was sent to me:

'Ever since I can remember I have had a tremendous interest in the supernatural, the paranormal, call it what you will. The origin of my interest was born on the first day of my arrival in our new home here twenty-two years ago.

'I was two years old when my family brought me to this house and from the beginning I was aware that we were not the only occupants of this house that I have grown to love very much.

'Naturally as a small child I would become alarmed at any occurrence that I could not understand, but as time has marched on, I have come to realise that without our faceless friends, life would not be the same.

'Allow me, if you will, to unfold some of the events that have happened to us all during our time here. The house itself was built around 1884, one of a block of four. It is an ordinary house, but at the time of its erection, it would have been viewed as a house for the middle-class, and we know for a fact that a "daily" was employed by the first occupants.

'This brings me to my next point. I carried out some enquiries as to the identity of those first occupants, the result of which supplied me with the family name and that of a sister of the then occupants, a Miss Sarah, a devout Quaker who dressed in a simple but practical fashion as befitting the time. According to the information I gained, Miss Sarah lived to a considerable age, she had a pronounced stoop and walked with a restricted shuffle.

'On my fifth birthday my mother put me to bed at six o'clock as usual and told me not to read but to go to sleep like a good girl. Since the day had been full of such new and exciting things, especially my new model pony and books, I just could not get off to sleep. So I put on my light and started to look at my new picture book. I must have been captivated by the book for some time before my interest was drawn from the book to my model pony on the cupboard beside my bed. Everything was so quiet that I can still recall the horror I felt as I watched the pony quite definitely move from one side of the cupboard to the other making an awful screeching, scraping sound as it went before falling or being flung to the ground. In my panic I could not move or say a word, let alone cry for help. After what seemed an age I managed to pull the bedclothes over my head and I remained there until I heard my mother open my door to see that all was well.

'When I tried to tell my mother what had happened she told me it must have been a draught, I must not be so silly and I must go to sleep. This incident was to be the first of many that puzzled me. On another occasion not very long after we had moved in my elder sister came to see us. Mother took her on a guided tour of the new homestead, my sister having with her a black poodle called Heidi that belonged to her mother-in-law. As the trio moved from room to room all seemed to be well until they reached the bathroom. This had once been a kitchen and a bedroom when the house had been converted into flats during the Second World War. As they approached the threshold of the bathroom Heidi began to whimper and drag her back legs. My sister tried to pull her through the door but Heidi broke free and shot down the stairs like a bullet from a gun, out through the kitchen to the safety of the back garden where my father was working in the shed.

'My sister was a little disturbed at this but carried on into the bathroom where she suddenly became aware of a presence, an icy atmosphere suddenly bringing the happy chatting to an abrupt end. Both my mother and sister looked at one another and made a hasty retreat from the room.

'On another occasion, when I had reached the age of about eight, I was again reading in my bedroom when the light went out. Not

Falmouth in the days when gaslights and ghosts seemed to go together.

being especially put out by this, I reached out for the switch and turned it back on. It did have a tendency to do this because my father had recently redecorated my room and the paint had made the switch a little stiffer than usual. As I picked up my book again the light went out once more. I was getting a little annoyed with this so once again I switched it on. It went out again and came on, went out and came on, all by itself; this went on for several seconds before I cried out for my mother.

'Mother was growing more than a little tired with my constant shouts for help during the evenings when I was supposed to be asleep, so she ran up the stairs, stormed into my bedroom and started to tell me off when the lights did their "disappearing' trick yet again. She made sure that the switch was off, closed my door and went to her own room. Moments later my light came on; not only that, the switch was making a most definite clicking sound, as if someone was flicking the switch with their finger. I cried out again but what I did not know was that my mother was experiencing the very same thing

A more modern view of the old Cornish port – but Falmouth maintains its strong supernatural reputation.

in her room next door. She came into my bedroom, held my hand and smoothed my hair until I was sound asleep. The next day my mother reported a fault in the system and an electrician called. Upon examination of the lights, wiring and switches, he announced that all was well and no repairs of any kind were required.

'Over the next two years the happenings, as we call them, were to get more regular and more spectacular. My father has a routine where he goes out every Saturday evening for a drink. About twelve years ago we always used the back door as our main entry point into the house. The front door was seldom used so we all became accustomed to the distinctive sound of the back door opening which was always preceded by the click of the latch being lifted on the back gate. Also in those days we would have our television set in the room which overlooked the back so we could always hear if anyone came in.

'However, one Saturday night, my mother, brother and myself were all sitting down watching the television. We all heard the back gate open and a man's footsteps come up the garden path, turn the handle on the back door and enter the kitchen. The time was around 9.30. We know this because mother remarked as she glanced at the clock that it was very early for father to have returned from the local. We heard the familiar sound of the coffee mugs being handled and moved; of this we took no notice, as it was my father's practice to bring coffee in for us when he came home. About twenty minutes had passed and there was still no sign of father or of the coffee, so my brother said he was going to see what Dad was up to.

'Within seconds he emerged from the kitchen, his face ashen, and he was visibly trembling; he told us that Dad was nowhere to be seen, the kettle was stone cold, the mugs unmoved and there was no sign of anyone having been in the kitchen at all.

'Dad did finally come home at around 11.00 and the first thing my mother asked him was had he returned home earlier in the evening. Of course his reply was no; in fact he had been to St. Mawes on the other side of the estuary with the Nankersey choir all evening; but we had all heard our visitor in the kitchen hours earlier . . .

'My father was always sceptical about the whole idea that there may be ghosts in our house but he soon became a firm believer after an experience, again in the bathroom. He had gone to the bathroom for his customary evening wash and shave. During the course of his ablutions he had heard someone come up the stairs and give a sigh of relief when they reached the top. He called out, thinking it was my brother messing around, but he received no reply and thinking no more about it, he turned back to the mirror to resume his shaving when someone or something breathed down the back of his neck, releasing a mournful groan while doing so . . . Needless to say Dad became very alarmed and left the bathroom with some speed!

'I have also encountered a strange happening in our bathroom. It has always been rather a gloomy place but on this particular winter evening it became, just for a moment, a wonderfully warm place, filled with a happiness that I have never felt in this house before or since. I was sitting in the bath, up to my neck in foam, thinking about what I was going to do that evening, when suddenly I became aware of a presence. The hairs on my arms stood up as if a small electrical charge had been passed through my limbs, and I felt as if I was being watched. I turned my head to face the airing cupboard on my left, and there before me stood this small figure, a woman with her hair scraped back very close to her head and wearing a long navy-blue skirt, reaching nearly to the floor, and with such a small waist that she looked as though she might snap in half at the first gust of wind.

'She looked just like anyone else in the physical sense, and she was smiling but the smile forced a horrible sensation through my body as she did not appear to have any teeth. So there she was, toothless grin and all, and I could not help but notice her carriage, a pronounced stoop; all this made me feel very uneasy, but somehow the atmosphere was one of calm and I felt no urge to panic; in fact quite the opposite. I looked away and when I looked again she had gone. I remember thinking that it must be Miss Sarah and I expect she is wondering what I am doing in her house . . . Bearing all this in mind, I no longer took any notice of the small shadowy figure that used to shuffle past the doors on the odd wintry evening.

'We have always had great difficulty in getting animals to enter our bathroom and it has always been a great source of amusement to our friends. Whenever the opportunity presents itself for us to try and get a new dog into that bathroom without success, we become even more convinced that this must be the nerve point of all the ghostly happenings that occur in our house.

'As I moved into the next stage of my development at around thir-

teen years of age the activity grew stronger in our house. My father was convinced that I was the focal point for all that went on, and tried to dissuade me from delving too deeply into the unknown. I collected all the information I could on the subject and spent many hours in my room reading . . . I remember I had one of your books that contained many stories about hauntings in houses all over the United Kingdom.

'The noise level in our house was tremendous for about twelve months with bangings, coughs and even scratching sounds coming from the corners of the rooms. On one particular occasion during the very hot summer of 1976, I was asleep when the hatch to the attic in my bedroom slid across, causing me to be showered in grit and dust. My father said it must have been the wind but since there was not a breath of wind that night, it seemed a feeble explanation to me. This happened several times and in the end my father nailed down the hatch and put up a false ceiling to prevent it happening.

'After that our visitor took to knocking at the bedroom door, with finger-nails, which was most upsetting for me. I would call out 'Come in' but nobody ever did. When I went to open the door to see if it was my brother fooling about, there was never anybody in sight, the house was in darkness and everything was silent and still.

'When I was about sixteen, my brother and I took to a crude method of trying to summon up the presence using a wine glass and letters of the alphabet cut from paper. This proved to be a disaster and a month of disturbances followed, much to the annoyance of our parents.

'We eventually called in a medium whom I had befriended at the local spiritualist church. She said that the presence was a friendly one and Richard, my brother, and I were very foolish to have tried to communicate with it as we had probably called up something very unfriendly indeed.

'We followed her advice and ceased our activities; thus peace and calm returned to the house for a while. Until, that is, I purchased a harmonium. I have always loved music, especially Sankey and Moody hymns, as indeed does my father – and so it seems, does the old lady . . . We spent many Sunday afternoons singing around the harmonium, enjoying its mellow tones.

'On several occasions, during our Sunday afternoon sessions, we heard a woman's voice singing with us. It was quite a shock at first but now it would not be the same without her. I am now twenty-four years old; I love our house very much; and I could not think of leaving it or our friend as she has become one of the family, so to speak. It would be a terrible shame if we were to sell up and the next owners got rid of her . . . after all, she was here long before we were and if I have my way, she'll remain here as long as she may wish to do so.

'As for the manly footsteps; well, we have not heard them since I was a small girl and I don't suppose we'll ever know who they belonged to. There have been many other happenings in this house, some nice and some not so nice. But whenever they happen at least now we are not at all bothered by them; indeed life would be very mundane and ordinary without them.'

In reply I said, 'How interesting that you seem to have ghostly activity that is confined to the house and its occupants and I am pleased to know that like most people in similar circumstances, you have come to terms with whatever entities there may be and live in harmony with them; ghostly encounters notwithstanding.'

* * * * *

The spirit trapped by fire
Gillingham, Dorset

A COUPLE of years ago I received a letter from the occupants of an historic house in Gillingham, to which I replied promptly and hoped to visit but for reasons that are unclear to me I heard no more about the matter. However, the case is such a singular one that I feel it more than merits inclusion in a volume devoted to ghostly encounters and I am quoting verbatim from the original letter sent to me, deleting or altering only details that might identify the actual premises.

'I have just bought and read your very interesting *Ghosts of Dorset* and it has prompted me to write this letter in the hope that you can help to explain my experiences.

'In July 1987 we had my brother visiting us for a while; Leslie is very sensitive and mentioned that he felt a presence at the top of The Oaks. Up until then I had ignored the local tales of the ghost in our house that seemed to be common knowledge. I made Leslie promise that he would not mention anything to William, our 14-year-old as I thought it would make him afraid to move about the house freely. I have to say that I had always sensed something but had lived in the house for a couple of years prior to Leslie's visit without any problems. At the end of July William went on holiday for three weeks.

'I was finding it difficult to sleep at the time, as each night I had what seemed like a frightening experience. I tried sleeping in different rooms but everywhere the same dream followed me. I must explain that The Oaks and The Laurels adjoin each other; we purchased them both and knocked them together as they were one house originally. Eventually I gave up trying to sleep and only felt safe in the living room dozing on the sofa. Below is exactly what took place during the next few days.

'On August 1 I tried sleeping in a room in The Laurels; Leslie was in a room down the passageway in the same house and I felt safe. I fell asleep fairly quickly. I thought I woke up and felt I had to turn on my bedside lamp. I reached for the switch as I turned my head but all I could see was the table, everything that should have been on it wasn't there, lamp, book, glasses, ashtray, etc. Thinking nothing of this I got out of bed to turn on the main light; I flicked the switch as I turned back towards the bed, nothing. I flicked the switch again, nothing. I shrugged as I got back into bed, thinking the bulb had blown. As I lay down in bed it felt as if something passed into me; I couldn't move and a feeling of dread was overwhelming. I tried to call out, to say a prayer or even what Leslie had advised me to say: the words "go away" came out as a distorted guttural sound. I tried desperately to get these words out and gradually whatever held me let me go and the words became clearer as I repeated them over and over again. I don't know if I was dreaming but I could hear the traffic outside, the wind rattling the window and our dog, Billie, moving about in his basket in my room (my moral support!!). Eventually I was calm again. I said a prayer and fell asleep, waking up as usual but bathed in sweat, very unusual for me as I am not prone to excess sweating. It was after this night in The Laurels that I took to sitting in the living room, frightened to fall asleep.

'August 10 found me once more in the living room, everyone else had gone to bed. At about 11.30 p.m. I thought I was being silly and decided to go to bed myself. Not wanting to disturb anyone I went into William's room, taking Billie the dog with me. I turned on the night light for moral support and got into bed, coaxing Billie onto the bed. I lay on my right side with my left arm resting on Billie. Sleep seemed to elude me and after a while I became uncomfortable and turned to stretch out flat on the bed. As I did this a force hit me, knocking my head leftwards; and almost at once I felt what I can only describe as a "whoosh" going into me, via my right ear. My whole body stiffened and I could not move, yet the muscles of my legs began to twitch. My eyes were open and I could see the movement of my legs under the bedclothes. I looked around the room but could not see anything – at the same instant Billie jumped off the bed and curled up in his basket.

'I struggled to regain control of my body but once more the sounds coming from me were guttural as I tried and tried to say "go away". After what seemed an age I won and kept repeating the words over and over. My watch said 2.20 a.m. and I found I could now raise my arm off the bed. I kept my eyes open and carried on speaking what had now become a chant: "Go away, go back to where you belong. Go away, go back to where you belong". As I lay there I turned on the night light. As I watched it started fading and then getting bright alternately. I was too scared to get out of bed and leave the room as the light was on a table by the door. All I did was carry on the chant louder and louder to give me confidence. Stan, my husband, heard me and came to the door and called to me. I asked him to come into the room and suddenly it was all over. I flew downstairs and refused to go to bed again; it was now 4 a.m. Eventually Stan persuaded me to come up to bed with the promise that he would keep watch while I grabbed a couple of hours sleep, but this was impossible. At 6 a.m. he went downstairs to make some coffee. I can only presume that in those few minutes I fell asleep because I experienced the same sensations as before.

'All the next day I was very nervous and what had seemed like a dream at first was now a real experience. That evening I fell asleep on the sofa while the family watched television. At about 11.00 p.m. Stan woke me up and I went to bed. Leslie went to bed at the same time, in his room in The Laurels. I had an undisturbed night for the first time in days.

'At 7 a.m. the next morning Stan woke me up – to inform me that Leslie had had a bad night. I came down quickly. Our kitchen is in The Laurels and Leslie and Stan were having coffee and I remember I could smell a faint smell of charred wood as I walked through from one house to the other.

'Leslie had gone to bed the night before and as he entered his room and sat down on his bed he was overcome by the smell of smoke. Thinking immediately of a fire he left his room and checked the whole of The Laurels but all seemed well and there was no smell of fire anywhere else. He went back towards his room but as he tried to enter the room he said he felt the room was on fire and he was nearly overcome by it; he withdrew and went downstairs and

Ghosts often appear in older houses such as these – perhaps because the ancient walls have soaked up the atmosphere and emotions of years and seen the lives and deaths of so many people.

the smell seemed to be all over the house now. Really frightened, he stepped through into The Oaks and found that all was well there. He spent the whole night in The Oaks, not wanting to disturb or frighten me any more. He tried all night, every hour, to get back into The Laurels but the heat and fumes drove him back each time . . .

'On the 12th August I telephoned the Psychic Association in London and related this tale; they advised me to get in touch with a Mr and Mrs South of Poole. Mrs South agreed to come down but she could not do so until the 13th. She advised us to isolate The Laurels and not sleep alone that night so Leslie doubled up with our older son in his room. We were trying to sort things out on the evening of the 12th at about 6.00 p.m.: coffee, tea, toaster etc., for breakfast the next morning before we shut up The Laurels for the night. For the first time Billie seemed to be behaving strangely. His ears pricked up and he ran to the bottom of the stairs wagging his tail; he stood there for a few moments and then flew up the stairs and sat down outside Leslie's room, whining to go in. We quickly got him down and locked up The Laurels, knowing that whatever it was was still there.

'On the 13th August Mr and Mrs South arrived at 2.00 p.m. and Leslie and I led them to his room. Leslie opened the door and they went in; we stood at the door looking into the room. Mrs South said, "Oh yes, she's here." As she said this the mirror on the wall started shaking, Leslie and I both witnessed this. Mrs South talked to "her" very patiently, persuading "her" to leave. I must say I felt very sad for "her", whoever "she" was. Mrs South said that "she" didn't want to leave, "she" wanted to stay in the house. Our ghost was a very strong lady and it took quite a while before she could be persuaded to leave.

'Mrs South said she was either a maid or a servant in the house, possibly as long ago as a hundred years; she had died in that room, trapped by fire which started in the room below; she even described her dress and her bed in the attic. We were told that her name was Sara.

'Things have been quiet since then, even though I personally still feel nervous when I'm on my own. I seem to have become more sensitive after my experience. My left leg, from the knee downwards prickles unreasonably in some environments and some nights even when I'm tucked up in a warm bed. I also experience a feeling on my left temple, akin to an insect crawling around in my hair but in the same spot, and no amount of brushing it off will take it away. Worst of all is that each night as I go to bed I get a tremendous flash in my head, sometimes so strong that it jerks my head sideways, accompanied by a sound like a twang of a guitar string. I am not asleep as I can hear all the sounds around me, i.e. hubby snoring! I lie quietly and my vision clears. I see a tunnel, lined with clouds, reddish in colour, I look down it, at the end is light and a blue sky.

'I see faces looking down at me, people I don't know, some are nice, some are evil which makes me open my eyes in fright. They come and go; I sense their moods but they never say anything. I sometimes go down to the end of this tunnel; I have only to think this and I am there, but the feeling of being drawn out of my body is very frightening and I always quickly open my eyes and make sure that I am still in bed . . . Maybe you have come across this sort of thing in your research? I hope that by understanding my experiences they won't frighten me so much. I have never doubted the supernatural but to have been able to experience the sort of power that "Sara" generated was an incredible experience.'

Well, as I have said, I replied promptly, hoping to visit and perhaps investigate this singular case of haunting but sadly I never heard any more. I can only hope that everything sorted itself out and that my correspondent is now at peace with all the inhabitants of her home.

* * * * *

The Grey Lady
Exeter, Devon

THE OLD Royal Devon and Exeter Hospital in Southernhay, Exeter, renamed Dean Clarke House, has a famous Grey Lady ghost which has haunted the hospital for many years.

The hospital, which dates back to 1741, was left a forlorn shadow of its former self in 1974, when all the doctors, nurses and patients moved away to the new general hospital at Wonford.

They left behind just a few caretakers – and the Grey Lady who, according to tradition, haunts the first floor corridor of the oldest part of the building. Until the early part of this century matrons of the hospital slept in a bedroom served by the corridor, and it is said that generations of nurses and doctors have seen the ghost there.

She is known as the 'Grey Lady' because of the grey uniform of an 18th century nursing sister that she is supposed to wear. Tradition says that she was always running along the corridor whenever anyone saw her.

If by chance she felt lonely for a while she can be lonely no more for the old hospital sprang back to life in 1977 as the headquarters of the Exeter Health Care District, and the Treasury of the Devon Area Health Authority, and nearly two hundred staff moved in.

The associate administrator of the Exeter Health Care District, Mr Alan Ruddock, said at the time: 'We have not seen the ghost yet, but we have heard a good deal about her. Her presence does not really bother us.'

Mrs Molly Alford, a former administrative sister, retired after thirty-six years of nursing in the hospital, said she had heard a good deal about the ghost too but she had never seen her personally. Miss Ruth Furze, a former matron, confirmed that until shortly after the Second World War the matron's bedroom was on the supposedly haunted corridor.

If the Grey Lady has not been seen in recent years, said Miss Furze, it was possible that she was smoked out by a fire which badly damaged the floor above in 1968. However, since I never heard of a ghost being destroyed by fire or even put off by smoke, I am not surprised to hear that the Grey Lady has in fact been seen several times in recent years.

A former nursing sister tells me that she saw the ghost one evening in 1973. At the time she recalls being struck by two things: firstly, the 'nurse' ahead of her in the long corridor was running – something nurses are taught *not* to do, and secondly, the 'nurse' was dressed all wrong: she was wearing a grey outdated uniform . . . This informant tells me that as these points went through her mind, the figure suddenly vanished and for the first time the viewer felt uneasy, frightened almost, for there was no way in which the figure could have disappeared from sight naturally.

Another witness I talked to, a former nurse, told me she had an almost identical experience some twenty years earlier. I understand that the 'haunted' corridor is now much changed but apparently the ghost still walks or rather runs on occasions in her accustomed place.

* * * * *

Midnight footsteps
Hullavinton, Wiltshire

CHIEF Inspector J. Sait contributed the following account to *Off Beat*, the newspaper for the men and women of the Surrey Constabulary and I am grateful to him for permission to use his article.

'I am reminded of an incident which, to this day, makes me wonder if there is a spirit world. I do not know sufficient to decide whether or not such things as ghosts exist, nor am I particularly keen on discovering firsthand! All I can say is what I experienced did happen, although what it was I cannot say.

'It was during early 1956, when I was in the Royal Air Force. I was stationed at R.A.F. Hullavinton, a Flying Training Command Station. One of the exercises pupil pilots were required to practice was known as "circuits and bumps". This was simply circuits of the airfield, followed by a touch down of the undercarriage, a short taxi and then off up into the air again.

'Because of the different levels of flying training, this exercise was extremely hazardous. The danger of accidents between the more and less experienced pupil pilots was accentuated by the frequent near misses. It was then decided that a disused station nearby should be renovated and used for this more dangerous phase of training.

'Part of the renovation involved the air traffic control tower and included the installation of valuable equipment. Until the station was fully operational it was necessary to mount a guard twenty-four hours per day. For this purpose, different airmen, in pairs, were to patrol and in the cases of the night duty, to sleep in the air traffic control building.

'I was one of the fortunates to be "selected" for a night guard. This particular night was the last before lighting equipment was to be installed. My co-guard and I patrolled the airfield, checking the out-buildings and eventually made our way back to the control tower, a building made entirely of concrete and steel.

'We entered the only door, securing it behind us. We made our way up the three floors, checking each room as we went. All without exception were locked, due to the equipment stored therein.

'On reaching the top floor, on which were our camp beds, we set-tled down for the night. The final duty was a telephone call which had to be put through at midnight. There was no need for both of us to remain awake so we tossed a coin to see who was to be the unlucky one – and I lost. As my co-guard settled down, the time by now being 11.30 p.m., I passed the time reading by the light of a torch.

'Shortly before 12 midnight, I heard the sounds of footsteps com-ing up the stairs. They were not clear sounds, but of a shuffling type; but footsteps they certainly were. They continued for several min-utes ending outside the door of the room in which my co-guard and I were.

'I should have awoken the other airman, but I am not ashamed to say that I could not move. I was as if almost petrified. I managed to switch off my torch and sat in the dark, hoping that whatever it was would not come through the door! After several minutes of silence I switched on my torch but everything was as it should have been. By now the time was midnight, so I left my bed and quietly crept to the telephone. I made the duty call, but made no mention of the foot-steps.

'I returned to my bed and very soon fell asleep. On wakening I asked my co-guard if he had heard anything unusual during the night, but he had not. Very soon our transport back to the main camp arrived and we left.

'On the run back I considered the possibility of having fallen asleep and dreamt the whole incident. I could not recall falling asleep between the time we locked the building and the time I made the telephone call. Nonetheless, I checked with the main Camp Guardroom and my phone call had been logged at midnight.

'What had made the noise of footsteps I could not imagine. The building was of steel and concrete. We had checked each room and window on each floor as we went back up the stairway. There was no other living creature in the building, yet something had walked up the stairs!

'I never pursued the history of the area or the ground on which the air traffic control tower had been built. For all I know someone may have died on that spot and to this day be walking around, and for some reason, only I was to be aware of it that night.

'I discounted the possibility of a practical joke, as there were no other keys available. Was it a ghostly encounter? Who knows?'

In September 1991 Chief Inspector Sait told me: 'It was a statement of fact but I can offer no explanation of the experience'.

* * * * *

Wiltshire: a beautiful and heavily haunted landscape.

The glowing monk
Martinhoe, west of Lynton, Devon

IS THE lane between Martinhoe Manor House and Woody Bay Hotel haunted by a monk-like figure? Five people who spent a holiday in the vicinity in 1989 certainly think so. I am indebted to Martin Kelsey, David R. Crawford, Lisa Crawford and Lorraine Fisher for firsthand details of the experience – and particularly the two young ladies who seem to have experienced a ghostly encounter they are unlikely ever to forget.

Paraphrasing David Crawford's account, the five young people: David Crawford, 26, his sister Lisa, 20, their brother Darran, 17, a friend, Lorraine Fisher, 21 and another friend, Terry Gibson, 28, were staying in cabins at Martinhoe Manor, in the Heddon Valley of North Devon when they decided one evening to walk up to the Woody Bay Hotel for a drink – they had *no* alcohol prior to the 'encounter' but, as David Crawford says, 'we certainly needed one afterwards!'

The dark and narrow track, bordered by trees and foliage, became narrower still and where there is a steep drop on the right-hand side, just past Inkerman Bridge – they could hear the rushing water but it was so dark they couldn't see a thing – Terry walked ahead with a torch and the rest linked arms for safety, the two girls together.

Suddenly, near some ancient, worn steps, one of the girls, Lorraine Fisher, felt a little tug on her cardigan and she asked who was fooling around but no one admitted touching her. When the same thing happened again, she again asked who was responsible but before anyone could answer her friend Lisa Crawford turned round and began screaming. Lorraine swung round too and they both saw a shape that resembled a monk wearing a black habit and hood. The hood completely hid the face and the figure seemed to be unusually wide. It seemed to glow, making it vivid and distinct in the pitch blackness. The figure seemed to the girls to be little more than a foot or two away and Lorraine screamed too and then closed her eyes hoping the form would disappear but when she opened her eyes again the form was still there, but now it was moving around as though looking for something. The boys turned to see what the girls were screaming at but none of them could see anything!

Lisa tells me the figure seemed to be about her own height, 5 feet 2 inches, but very wide. At first it seemed almost on top of her and she 'screamed uncontrollably and turned round in terror'. The boys were at a complete loss and Terry flashed his torch around, but saw nothing to account for the girls' sudden and very real terror. Lisa said the form seemed to 'glow black', the lower half of the hooded head seemed white but no features at all were discernible. By the time the girls had calmed down sufficiently to be able to explain what they had seen, the wide, monk-like form was no longer visible to either of the girls.

A friend who visited the area the following year was shown a photograph taken by a resident of Rugeley, Staffordshire, of the same area of pathway and depicting a monk-like figure. Both girls say this representation is nothing like the form they saw. Was this ghostly encounter experienced by the two female members of the party present and invisible to their three male companions? Much paranormal activity is experienced when it is least expected; tactual phenomena is not unknown and yet, one is left with so many unanswered questions . . .

That the girls saw something seems indisputable. David Crawford tells me: 'When we eventually reached Woody Bay we were all badly shook up and the girls were in a state of shock. They decided, quite understandably, that they couldn't face going back down that track on the way home. So Terry, Darren and I were faced with the task of going back to the manor for Terry's car either one of two ways: the long way round, or down the track. The thing we did then may be the bravest thing we have ever done! Armed with only a torch we decided to follow the track and be ready for anything . . . as it happened we didn't see a thing – much to our relief. We got the girls home safely and told our other friends at the manor. Martin and

his uncle, Steve, accompanied Darren and me down the track that night and many nights after in the hope of catching a glimpse (and even a photograph) of the ghost, but to no avail. Lisa, Lorraine and Terry wouldn't walk down there again at night.

'The first person we mentioned the event to, a lady behind the bar, shortly after we had composed ourselves that night, showed some surprise (but no obvious disbelief) that the track should be haunted as the chef had walked his dog along there for the past ten years or so and had never reported anything unusual.

'We all racked our brains to find a logical explanation and although there was no noticeable variation in temperature we can only conclude that it was a ghost. Our friends, who we trust anyway, couldn't have planned it as a trick because they didn't know we would walk to Woody Bay Hotel that night; they didn't know we would take that route and they didn't know we would go at that time. Besides, the path was gravelly and for someone to creep up on us so silently and then disappear into thin air would really take some doing! We thought about the old steps; could someone have come down them when we had passed? It has to be very doubtful as the first step is some height off the ground and even in daylight it is considerably difficult to find and climb them. A person would have had to jump off the step and that would have made quite a noise.'

As far as is known the man who photographed the track in daylight and obtained one shot that shows a slim, white, transparent, monk-like form had no knowledge of any reputed ghost or of the track being 'haunted' – but putting on one side the curious photograph there is still the strange, quite terrifying and extremely puzzling experience of the party of young holidaymakers that autumn evening in 1989.

* * * * *

The lost souls
Nether Lypiatt, Avon

THE MANOR house at Nether Lypiatt, near Stroud, home of the Prince and Princess Michael of Kent has a ghost, if not two, and both members of the Royal Family took part in a religious ceremony a few years ago to exorcise the place and to banish an evil spirit from the 300-year-old house.

The Prince and Princess, worried about tales of an annual visit by the ghost of a young blacksmith, assisted two priests, one Roman Catholic and the other Anglican, in sprinkling holy water in every room in the house, the day before the annual visit was due.

The blacksmith was hanged by a previous owner of the house, Judge Charles Coxe, and his ghost is said to return on the anniversary of the execution. Neither the Prince nor the Princess are usually at home on January 25 when the ghost is said to appear, perhaps consciously or maybe coincidentally. 'He appears every year and he's very charming,' businessman Frederick Nettlefold insists. He owned the property before it was bought by the royal couple. The nearest neighbour, Mrs Jane Wood, said, 'I have never seen the ghost but I have heard that he rides past the house across the courtyard on a big, white horse.'

Charles Coxe ordered the hanging of the blacksmith for stealing sheep in 1704 but he promised the man a pardon if he would make a perfect pair of gates for the front of the Nether Lypiatt estate.

The blacksmith toiled day and night for two weeks 'as if driven by the Devil himself' (according to the legend), but when they were completed the unforgiving judge spotted a small flaw in the top right-hand corner and, decreeing that the weary and hard-working blacksmith had not produced a *perfect* pair of gates, the unfortunate man was taken away and hanged. Soon afterwards the judge was found dead in nearby Toadsmoor Wood.

According to the legend and there is some evidence that it does occur, every January 25, at midnight, the gates of the mansion burst open and the ghostly form of the blacksmith appears, his face deathly pale, riding a white horse. He gallops three times round the courtyard in front of the house and then rides off.

The house is also reputed to be haunted by the ghost of a lady in white who walks through the ornamental gardens occasionally, at no set time or date. Who she is and why she haunts no one seems to know.

Previous owners of the property, Simon and Suna Boyle, found the 20-room mansion an unlucky and distinctly haunted house. They were continually worried by sights and sounds in the house that they were totally unable to explain and it all made things very difficult for their marriage and later they were divorced. A leading exorcist said at the time that he 'wasn't very happy about the atmosphere in the house' and he felt 'there may be lost souls wandering about there.' Had he been asked to do so he would have been 'obliged to deliver the house of souls, i.e. conduct an exorcism'.

A local investigator said in 1984: 'It's a very eerie place, especially at night. We went with friends to watch for the ghost. A psychic came with us and she was convinced that there was a ghostly presence.'

According to the royal couple's private secretary the ceremony at which the Prince and Princess were present was a simple blessing but it seems they did not wish to risk the possibility of a ghostly encounter with the ghostly blacksmith.

* * * * *

Ghosts and churchyards seem to have a logical and natural affinity.

Family phantoms
Newnham-on-Severn

DONALD Armstrong, MBE, former British Vice-Consul in Algarve, tells me that before he was married he lived with his parents in an early Georgian house in Newnham-on-Severn, a property consisting of a ground floor and two upper floors.

There was a fine staircase in the house which people were always admiring and one rather persistent American really wanted to buy it. If he could, he promised to replace it with an excellent modern one, but Mr Armstrong senior refused.

One evening in the early 1950s Donald was lying in bed reading when he felt a heavy weight land on his feet. Thinking it was his long-coated dachshund he said, 'Helga, you bad girl . . .' but the dog was not in the room and there was no sign of anything to account for the experience.

Next day, when he told his mother of the curious incident, she said, by way of reply, that once, recently, when she was in bed she had felt her shins tapped sharply: there was no explanation.

One night Donald was out to dinner with some friends and he returned home around midnight. In order not to disturb his parents, he tiptoed up the very ancient circular back stairs to the top floor where his room was situated. Next day his father asked him, somewhat sharply, 'Why did you have to run up the stairs last night past our door?' When Donald said that in fact he had not done so and had purposely used the back stairs, his father told him that the running steps had passed up the main stairs about twenty minutes past two in the morning.

On one occasion, at the same house, Donald's aunt came down one afternoon and said she had just left the Blue Room when she saw a figure that seemed to be composed of rolling smoke, in the shape of a woman in a crinoline going down the staircase and entering the Music Room on the first floor. She immediately followed and found the room empty.

Mr Armstrong had several other ghostly encounters, both in England and abroad. When he was a child the family used to stay with friends of his grandparents who had a huge house on the shores of Windermere, called Ecclerigg. At Christmas time, either 1930 or 1931, Donald, eight or nine at the time, was in his room asleep and was awoken by a terrible noise as if a bunch of madmen were throwing furniture about downstairs. He looked at his watch and saw it was about two o'clock in the morning. His first thought was that the maids were turning out the rooms below until he realised that this was highly unlikely at such an hour. Then he thought the adults (his parents and host and hostess) were making the noise as they came to bed but the noise was so loud that such an explanation was unthinkable.

Then, quite suddenly, he felt great fear and when he somewhat recovered he eventually tiptoed to his parents' room where he found them fast asleep. He lay down on the mat between the beds and spent the rest of the night there. In the morning he woke up and left the room before his parents were awake. 'Being an odd child,' he told me, 'I said nothing about this strange happening until the Christmas of 1940 when I was on leave from OCTU and I started to tell the story when we were chatting with some friends. My mother stopped me at the beginning and said, "Let me finish, this happened to me when I was a child in the first decade of the century in Ecclerigg". She had had an identical experience.'

Donald Armstrong went on to say that his father sold his companies in 1963 while Donald was farming in Kenya and he bought a house in Clare in Suffolk, a house that had been built in 1506. 'A lovely home but a disturbed house. The breakfast room had a low ceiling and sometimes heavy footsteps sounded in the boxroom above. I was in England once when this happened at breakfast and we had a friend staying with us. I said to John, "Put your hand on the ceiling" for I had noticed before that when the footsteps sounded you could actually feel the vibrations, and I then tiptoed up the

small backstairs and opened the boxroom door. The room where the footsteps sounded was full of trunks and nothing else. John said the noise had stopped as he heard me open the door. We both decided that the sounds resembled those of a man in heavy boots packing things in boxes, preparatory to moving perhaps. There were steps up and down the room and then the sound of something being dragged along the floor, just as though a box was being pulled across the room. It all went on for some time and was heard on many occasions but we never discovered any explanation.

'On the same leave I woke one night around two in the morning. I remember it was a bright moonlit night and as I listened to discover what had awakened me, I could hear the distinct sounds of boots on the gravel of the drive outside. I quietly got out of bed and looked out of the window. There was nobody there. I even shone my powerful torch onto the ground but the drive was completely deserted. I had thought a policeman might have come to check the door or something but no living person was there. My friend John heard it too. The steps kept on, up and down the drive, just a few feet below my window, for several minutes. We never discovered what caused them or why.

'On another occasion an old friend of the family, Major Thompson, a totally practical man, was staying at the house. One morning he said to my mother, "Who was on the run last night?" Apparently he had heard hurrying footsteps passing his door several times towards the lavatory over a period of about ninety minutes. In fact nobody had been "on the run".

'In 1965, after Independence in Kenya, I went to live in Algarve. I was married and had a daughter. We had this old Portuguese house in Praia da Rocha, bungalow-type and about sixty years old. In 1983, when my daughter was nine, the marriage broke up and my daughter went to live with her mother, about twenty minutes drive away. I was British Vice-Consul in Algarve at the time and my daughter, whom I worshipped, would come and stay with me every weekend – but she never came again after the noises started.

'I lived alone and my maid came every morning. One Christmas night I came in about 10.30 and was undressing for bed. I was alone in the house at the time. Suddenly the devil's own noise started in the roof space above my bedroom. Banging, thudding . . . I never heard anything like it, before or since. It was so violent that flakes fell from the ceiling. Suddenly one of the doors leading to the kitchen slammed shut with a crash that shook the house. I was standing nearby but it hadn't moved! It was quite horrible and so frightening and persistent that eventually I went outside and dossed down in the car for the night. There are only two ways of entering the roof, both trapdoors and both were screwed down. I examined them the next day and they hadn't been touched for years. The same thing happened that summer and I moved into the front bedroom.

'The last time I stayed in the house was 1987 and one night I was cleaning my teeth at 10.30 before going to bed. The bathroom door to the kitchen corridor was open when there was a loud crash close beside me like a revolver going off. I shouted, "Who's there?" Nothing. The bang was just as though a powerful leaf spring had been pulled and then released against a wooden door; as if power had slowly built up and then exploded. I was frightened, I admit it. Every time it happened I checked the doors and windows. I have been through the sharp end of a war for six-and-a-half years and farmed alone in Kenya during Mau Mau but I have never been so frightened as I was in my home in Praia da Rocha. Had somebody been with me I could have appreciated it, but I was very afraid of something actually appearing. The house is now pulled down to make way for a vile high-rise block . . . All of this is absolutely true. My beloved Algarve dog, George, twice refused to use the corridor to the kitchen when called for his supper but preferred to go into the garden and round the patio to the kitchen door.'

* * * * *

The grieving ghost
Newton Abbot, Devon

A LADY living near Exeter read my *Ghosts of Devon* last year and says it inspired her to relate her experiences while living at Newton Abbot some twenty years ago. She writes:

'When my husband and I moved from Salcombe to Newton Abbot in 1971 I was six months pregnant and my initial "uneasiness" about the house was put down to my being unwell during this time. With hindsight, the whole house had a very musty, old smell to it even though it had been re-decorated prior to our moving in; also, when standing in the hallway our eyes were invariably drawn upstairs as if a "shadow had moved . . ."'

'We chose the bedroom at the front of the house, putting our little daughter into the adjoining back bedroom. Invariably she woke sometime in the night to say our Labrador was in her room – mistakenly. When our second daughter was about six months old, we put both little girls in the same room, hoping Julia would sleep more contentedly; but no – she still had disturbed nights. We then thought of actually changing bedrooms and this had the desired effect.

'Then, one night towards the end of one of my husband's weeks of night duty, I awakened to find "someone" quite solid standing at one side of our bed dressed in a white sweater. I was extremely cold and it was deathly quiet, even when "it" crossed its arms in front to take the sweater off!! There was no sound whatever. Even though I knew it was not my husband I still said, "Is that you?" and "it" looked at me – it seemed to have "floppy" cheeks I remember – and then it disappeared. I could see our wardrobe again . . .

'My husband arrived home less than an hour later. I ran downstairs and told him what had happened. He, like me, was in no doubt that I had seen a ghost . . .

'A few months later we had an elderly lady medium come to the house to see whether she could tell us anything about "our friend". By the time she reached our upstairs landing she was crying her heart out and later she said it was a very strong experience. Apparently "he" was grieving all the time for his mother who had been buried in Highweek Cemetery, and he would go from the vicinity of our spare bedroom through our bathroom to the back bedroom (where originally our daughters had slept and now, my husband and myself) and look out longingly at that place.

'She also said "his" house was a large old red-brick place with a corridor where our bedroom was now situated; but our house had only been built for approximately ten years at that time. Apparently he would also sit downstairs, she said, pointing to a corner of our sitting room, still grieving, and looking towards Highweek.

'The only little bit of research we did was to try and find out about the original house, the one that we supposed had once occupied the site before our house was built; but we were told there was no such place . . . Then, about twelve months later, South Western Electricity Board decided to demolish their cooling tower which was situated across the mud flats from the back of our house and there, in direct line and now visible from our back bedroom was Highweek Cemetery. The medium told us too that the ghost's name was Rupert Williams; perhaps I'll do some research into that one day . . .'

* * * * *

64

Bossiney book illustrator Felicity Young and her dog Arthur explore a haunted location in Devon, high on Dartmoor.

On the road
Nunney, Somerset

A T A meeting of the Ghost Club which was addressed by Michael Goss on the subject of *The Evidence for Phantom Hitch-Hikers*, we talked about the curious Nunney case.

Three miles southwest of Frome, the attractive little village has become something of a mecca for would-be ghost-seers after a 'middle-aged' phantom was repeatedly reported to be seeking to hitch lifts on the road leading to Frome – and then disappearing.

An early report came from a 20-year-old decorator who claimed he had picked up a man wearing a check jacket on the Frome-Nunney road. The man had climbed into the back seat of the car and the driver locked the door on him. Apparently the only remark made by the traveller was to the coldness of the weather. Almost immediately a question from the driver elicited no response and when he turned round, he found the traveller had disappeared although he had heard no sound of any kind. The puzzled driver, worried that his unidentified passenger might have been injured alighting from a moving car, reported the matter to the local police – who promptly gave him a breathalyzer test: he had not been drinking.

Shortly afterwards the same young man claimed to have undergone a second encounter with the same individual – at approximately the same place. This time the 'middle-aged man' was standing in the middle of the road and the driver had to skid to a sudden halt when he came upon the 'man'. When he got out of his car the person he had clearly seen and recognized as the man to whom he had previously given a lift, had completely disappeared.

'… a middle-aged phantom seeking to hitch lifts …'

News of this second encounter and further stories of somewhat dubious origin prompted local residents to form what came to be called the Nunney Vigilantes who patrolled the area with noise detectors, tape recorders, light meters and cameras, under the leadership of Ron Macey (who actually lived on the haunted road) but, perhaps predictably, they had no success in obtaining evidence of the 'phantom hitch-hiker'.

The local police then came forward with news of an accident resulting from a driver swerving to avoid a man in the road and they readily admitted that on 'several occasions' drivers had arrived at the police station 'in a state of virtual hysteria' reporting vanishing figures on the same stretch of road. Police and local residents were intrigued by the idea that the 'hitch-hiker' might be the ghost of an American serviceman killed in a car crash in the identical area.

Margaret Royal told me that she traced three separate motorists who, late at night, had picked up a man who subsequently inexplicably vanished on the Nunney road. One had reported the matter at Frome Police Station and another had gone to hospital for treatment for shock. Each motorist referred to the 'man' as 'between forty and fifty and wearing a check jacket'.

At the height of the publicity surrounding the appearances a former lorry-driver, George Gardiner, came forward to reveal that years earlier he could recall one or two of his fellow-drivers reporting seeing what might well have been the same ghostly figure in the same area of roadway. He added that his understanding at the time had been that a cyclist had been knocked down by a motorist at the 'haunted' spot and his appearance was the result of his dying curse on all motorists.

Mr Owen Hillier, a resident of Nunney for over fifty years, said he had heard his father talk of the ghost and, he believed, his father's father too. His recollection was that the ghost appearances concerned an innocent man hanged for the murder of his wife.

Whatever the explanation 'frequent' reports of vanishing hitchhikers on this stretch of road resulted in several police searches being made along the road – all unfruitful. The Nunney case is a good illustration of how very difficult it can be to establish a ghost sighting but if we feel there is no unassailable evidence that the Frome to Nunney road was ever haunted in the way reported then we are left with the awkward question of why motorists would attempt to hoax the police with so unlikely a tale as that of a vanishing passenger and all so convincingly that the police instigated searches and preserved reports. Similar conflicting evidence pervades many reported ghostly encounters.

* * * * *

The figure in the window
Roche, Cornwall

I HAVE written briefly elsewhere about Roche Rock (*Ghosts of Cornwall*, Bossiney Books, 1983) detailing some of the curious happenings experienced in that curious 14th century cell, 680 feet above sea level, in which St. Roche himself is said to have lived and died. Thereafter it was, reputedly, occupied by successive saints. It is supposed to be the cell wherein the damned soul of Tregeagle tried to find sanctuary when he was pursued by fiends from Dozmary Pool ...

In March 1988 I received a letter from an inhabitant of Warminster who writes: 'Reading your enjoyable books has awakened memories of my own personal ghost story and I hope you may find it interesting. I may say that I wrote to the Society for Psychical Research soon after the event and they replied that they had no record of anything unusual at this place.' (*The Ghost Club has records extending over many years of curious happenings at Roche Rock! P.U.*)

'The event in question occurred about five years ago, probably in September. My boyfriend at that time was the adventurous type and he was much into risking life and limb on rocks, ruins and the like. We were in the habit of going camping or hiking for weekends and it was while returning from one of these jaunts that we stopped at Roche Rock.

'Roche Rock, as you know, is a granite outcrop near the quarries a few miles north of St Austell. The "monastery" is an impressive ruin, built into, on to and up from a massive granite block. It is currently little more than a shell, access being by means of metal ladders bolted to the walls.

'We had discovered this place a few years previously with some friends. Mark (my boyfriend) loved it because it was so climbable and yet rather risky. I was less keen, as it always seemed cold there and felt decidedly unsafe to me.

'On this occasion we climbed the first ladder and looked around. Mark decided he was going for a scramble round the ruin and I looked around for a few minutes, while some other visitors passed me and went down; then I shouted to Mark that I was going back to the car because I felt so cold; he replied that he would be down in a few minutes. I climbed down very quickly and I was really cold in the lower "room" and felt a very unwelcoming atmosphere; in fact I remember running back to the car although I don't really know why. After ten minutes or so there was no sign of Mark – not that that was an especially unusual occurrence. Feeling a little warmer, I walked back to the monastery thinking I would take some photographs of Mark at the top.

'As I approached I could see a figure in the windows so I took a couple of photos and then waved. There was no response which I thought distinctly odd. As I wound the camera spool on ready to take another picture from a closer viewpoint, I saw an unmistakable figure on the very top, waving. I took a photograph of Mark, then looked back at the window and the silhouetted figure was still there and I realised that whoever it was could not be looking out of the window as there are no floors there, or ceilings for that matter. As I realised this I took another photograph and turned to go towards the ladder, feeling very puzzled, somewhat reluctant and sincerely hoping that someone else would be up there with Mark. I found however that I simply could not climb the ladder; it was too cold, so I called to Mark to hurry and I am ashamed to say I then turned and fled back to the car!

'When Mark eventually returned I asked him if he had seen anyone else on the rock and when he replied in the negative, he then asked me why I had been staring at the window when he was on the top. I told him what I thought I had seen and he laughed it off.

'There is a kind of sequel to all this which is really what convinced me that I was not imagining things. A few weeks later I took the film to be developed and all three shots of Roche Rock were blank, nothing on the film or negative. My camera is the basic sort, without lens caps or anything fancy. All the preceding shots were fine, better than my usual efforts in fact, and subsequent shots were all present.

'This may all seem very trivial and circumstantial to you but to me the strongly hostile feeling on that sunny afternoon was very real and it left me feeling anxious for several days afterwards. I know nothing about Roche but after reading the accounts of hauntings in your book I just wonder whether it is one of those places which has absorbed an atmosphere from the past, something of the monks or people who lived there; if so all I can say is that they must have been a miserable lot!'

* * * * *

* *The climbing of Roche Rock is now strictly forbidden.*

'… one of those places which has absorbed an atmosphere from the past …'

Screams in the night
St. Briavels, Avon

A COUPLE of years ago Mr George Smith of Chichester who describes himself as 'a graduate chemist not given to flights of fancy' sent me an account of his experiences while staying at St. Briavels Youth Hostel, ten miles north of Chepstow in the Forest of Dean a few years previously. 'It may not seem a great deal in print,' he says. 'But it frightened me at the time and I have been careful not to embroider the story in any way . . . you may perhaps care to spend some time at the castle itself.'

Once again I cannot do better than quote from my correspondent's original account. The Youth Hostel in question occupies part of what was once a 12th century castle.

'The hamlet of St. Briavels stands on the top of the eastern bank of the River Wye in the Forest of Dean and can have changed little in the last thousand years. I have good cause to remember it.

'It was the second day of our holiday. My wife and I were walking the Offa's Dyke footpath that wanders in and out of the border between England and Wales for a distance of around a hundred and seventy miles.

'For its first ten miles, from the southern end, the path clings to the steep wooded side of the river valley with the torrent spinning and frothing below. It is no distance between St. Briavels and Chepstow but the places are worlds apart in character. The latter is a stopping-off point for the traffic across the Severn Bridge and is a bustling market town full of life. The former is a backwater, a hang-

Trees often feature in dreams and ghost stories. Wooded places such as the Forest of Dean keep their mystery – yet some people claim to find a source of healing energy in fine old trees such as these.

over from the middle ages and barely scrapes an existence.

'It was midsummer and hot. Patches of steamy mist which had never cleared from the valley hung around the tops of trees and the air was still and oppressive. The river is old there too and meanders continually so that the distance walked is double that one might expect from a cursory glance at the map. As a consequence, although we had set off from Chepstow early that morning we were very tired when we eventually began the climb through meadows out of the valley towards the village, pursued by a horde of biting insects.

'The village of St. Briavels turned out to be just a few houses bisected by a highway. There was a church, a shop and, incongruously, a castle complete with moat and drawbridge!

'The castle was probably built just after the Norman conquest but there is no historical reference to it until the year 1131 at which time the castle was in the ownership of the Sheriff of Gloucester, reputedly a nasty piece of work, Milo Fitz-Walter, who was accused of "oppressing the people" in his eagerness to extract the crown taxes. There is a local legend that the Countess of Hereford freed the tenants from Milo's excesses by bareing all, Lady Godiva style, to clear their debts. During the 13th century the castle was frequently used by King John as a hunting lodge and it has been in continuous occupation to the present day. It is now used by the Youth Hostel Association and it was there we had arranged lodgings for the night.

'Even down in the valley we had heard the church bells ringing. Normally I like the sound of church bells but there was no tune to the peal that day, just a continuous monotonous tolling. When we eventually reached the village each house we passed seemed to have a small group of locals standing in front who stopped gossiping and watched as we silently trudged past. No doubt they were merely curious to see sweating and dishevelled backpackers but at the time I remember feeling that we were intruding . . . I could sense their eyes on the back of my head even as we crossed the authentic drawbridge and booked ourselves in for the night.

'The inside of the building had been converted so that internally it had all the trappings of a conventional hostel. There was the usual bustle of activity with people taking off boots in the hall; the smell of cooking from the members' kitchen; the sound of beds being made upstairs . . . There was nothing to raise the slightest disquiet but I recall that I felt uneasy in a way that is difficult to explain.

'If I had not been so tired I might have spent some time reading up on the building, learning something of its considerable history and perhaps exploring. As it was, after an early tea, I said "good-night" to my wife and went to bed.

'The mens' dormitory was, and probably still is, located over the castle's dungeon and the narrow windows look out across the road to the church and graveyard. I must have fallen asleep quickly because I don't remember anything until I awoke with the church bell chiming midnight. I was in an upper bunk and I sat up and looked around wondering what had awoken me. Most of the other bunks were also occupied.

'I realised that it seemed to have turned cold and I felt anxious although there was nothing seemingly amiss. After a few moments, silent but for the quiet breathing of my fellow hostellers, I heard what I presumed was the distant sound of revellers returning from a late night at the local public house.

'As the voices became clearer it was apparent that what I had taken for singing was some sort of chant and to my ears a cruel chant. It was interspersed with low laughter and it rose and fell with a fairly regular rhythm. Then things started to happen in the dormitory.

'The man in the bunk below mine began to toss and turn. His breathing became progressively heavier until he almost choked and fought to get his breath. Then I was startled by a sudden noise from the bed opposite. Quietly at first, the occupant began to talk to himself. He seemed to be engaged in an argument that became more and more heated as the noise outside the window increased. None of what he said, however, seemed to make any sense to me.

'The chanting from outside was now right below the dormitory window. I remember wondering why the commotion outside had not awakened anyone. I had a sense that something unpleasant was about to happen; that tense feeling of expectancy I had last experienced prior to a street gang fight I had once witnessed as a teenager. The hair on the nape of my neck began to rise and I started to shiver. Then the chanting stopped. And the disturbance around me stopped too. Two or three more silent seconds passed.

'I decided against my better judgement to look out of the window but as I made to get out of bed the silence was broken by a scream like an animal in great pain. Immediately afterwards there was a cheer from those assembled outside followed by callous laughter.

'Then there followed a long slow scream. The scream of a young girl that built up from nothing until the castle walls seemed to vibrate with the sound.

'I shall never forget that scream. Somebody was in mortal terror. It went on and on as if the person screaming was being subjected to increasing levels of pain. Then it died off suddenly with a sob.

'I had virtually frozen when I heard the animal scream but I now forced myself to go to the window and look out. The full moon shone down on an empty courtyard. I could see the full length of the road in both directions. There was nobody out there.

'That was the end of the evening's entertainment but I lay awake for the rest of the night and was never more pleased to see the first light of dawn.

'At breakfast I thought I would make a point of asking everyone whether they had been disturbed during the night but after getting a few funny looks, I gave up. I was beginning to think I had had too much sun the day before when a girl in the kitchen asked if anyone had heard screaming during the night. She was the only other person in the hostel, including my wife, to have heard anything.

'The early morning mist was sprawling across the Wye valley below us when we set off with the village and castle in bright sunshine. I never took any pictures and I never looked back. Before we left I asked the warden whether, in the years he had lived there, he had seen or heard anything untoward. He didn't know what I was talking about although I overheard him telling an elderly gentleman from my dormitory that the castle was said to be haunted.

'I have never believed in ghosts but I do believe in evil and I know that something evil was abroad that night. Perhaps the evil that men do does live on, forever imprinted in the stones of castle walls, waiting to retell tales to a receptive mind. It may even have been the voice of the Countess of Hereford herself, all those years ago, suffering on behalf of Milo's tenants; who knows?

'Recently I came across a reference to the castle in a book about the Forest of Dean. It said that carved on the dungeon walls below the dormitory where I had so briefly slept are the words: THE DAY WILL COME THAT THOU SHALT ANSWER FOR IT. It is my intention never again to be in the position of "answering for it" on behalf of those lords of the manor long dead.'

Mr Smith ends his letter by saying that this is the only time any-

'*The scream of a young girl* …'

thing like this ever happened to him and, he says: 'You may like to add the story to your files and even visit the castle; I personally have no wish ever to go back there.'

*　*　*　*　*

A wistful ghost
South Hams, Devon

IF THE ruins of haunted Oldstone Hall in the quiet hamlet of South Hams could talk, they would tell of murder as well as ghostly encounters.

The hall was completed in the early days of the 18th century, being built on the site of a monastery by the Cholwich family, local wool merchants, who lived here for many years. It was a beautiful house in those days with three lakes in the grounds, a grotto, several secret tunnels and a hermit's cave – traces of all these can still be found. However the Cholwich family fell upon hard times and the house was sold to Percy Dimes, who had once been a steward of the Cholwichs.

Such are the twists of fate and it was while Percy Dimes was enjoying the life of a squire that a terrible disaster occurred. Dimes' beautiful daughter, Laura, fell in love with a young New Zealander named Hugh Shortland who was training to become a barrister, but he did not find favour with Laura's parents.

Mr and Mrs Dimes were not convinced that the plausible, dashing and admittedly presentable immigrant was a good match for their daughter and they forbade Hugh to enter the grounds of Oldstone Hall. Soon the couple were meeting clandestinely in nearby woods where they strolled hand in hand beside Monk's Pond. And soon they married secretly with Laura still living with her parents, certain that she would eventually be able to talk them round to accepting Hugh.

One day, after taking her home after a ride, Hugh left her as usual

'… *her drowned body was found, bolt upright, beneath the hat* …'

at the gates of the Hall and Laura wandered off into the woods for a walk by herself – and she never returned. Hours later, during a search, her riding hat was seen seemingly floating a few inches above the waters of Monk's Pond, quite near the bank. Then her drowned body was found, bolt upright, beneath the hat and soon Hugh Shortland was arrested on suspicion of murder. At the resulting trial he defended himself brilliantly, he was acquitted and the mystery of Laura's death was never solved.

The sudden, mysterious and untimely death of Laura hit her family hard; the house never seemed the same without her and in fact the family always said that she hadn't really left and the whole family without exception were convinced that the ghost of Laura Dimes haunted the house she loved. Even a chimney sweep, visiting the house, saw the ghost of Laura Dimes in what became known as The Ghost Room.

Ten years after Laura's death a mysterious fire destroyed Oldstone Hall and the only room left intact was The Ghost Room. Today her ghost haunts the ruins of the house where once she was happy and people living nearby are convinced they have seen Laura's ghost, perhaps seeking retribution for her murder; perhaps seeking to right some wrong that she had done; perhaps looking for the love of her life. Whatever the reason those who have encountered the ghost of Laura Dimes at Oldstone Hall seem to become affected with the wistful sadness that seemingly exudes from this lonely ghost in her lonely haunt.

*   *   *   *   *

The soldier spirit
Southleigh, Devon

SOME fifteen years ago a family named Downs moved from Yorkshire to their new home in Southleigh, Devon. Nicholas Downs, wine producer, his wife Helen, son Ian and daughters Sheena and Emma, all soon realised that they had moved into a haunted 17th-century farmhouse.

Teenager Sheena was the first to say she was aware of a 'presence' in the house; shortly afterwards her younger sister Emma noticed it too and then Mrs Helen Downs became aware of 'something' in the house other than the human occupants. The family pet dog had acted strangely ever since they had moved into the house, frequently acting as though it was aware of something invisible to its human companions. And then it refused to enter one room where the family felt the ghost lingered.

One day a visitor who had not been told of the odd feelings experienced by the occupants of the house, suddenly described a frightening encounter with a man dressed in old-fashioned military uniform . . . and then there was the night when Sheena was awakened at three o'clock in the morning by the sound of heavy breathing which continued, close to her, until she switched on her bedside lamp. The breathing sound ceased immediately and there was nothing to account for what she had heard.

Two weeks later Sheena's mother had an almost identical experience. Then one night, also at three o'clock in the morning, Emma revealed that she had been awakened by a weight pressing on her stomach. When she put her light on she saw that a heavy picture had been moved across the room while she had been asleep; a few nights later she was again awakened about the same time and as she switched on the lamp she saw a book 'floating through the air . . .'

The dog became more and more agitated in the vicinity of the bedroom where some of the disturbances took place and a presence there was felt by all the family; Emma in particular 'became a bag of nerves' (to quote her mother). 'She is frightened of being alone anywhere upstairs,' she said at the time and decided that it might be best if the girls slept together.

That same night Emma awoke again at three o'clock with the feeling of a dreadful weight on her chest. She awakened Sheena who said afterwards: 'We heard a curious, high-pitched sound, like you get from a radio that is not tuned in . . . I sat up and shouted at the ghost to leave Emma alone. Almost immediately I was slapped hard across the face . . .'

The family called in a priest from Exeter. The Rev. John Wheaton of the Liberal Catholic Church performed a two-hour exorcism and cleansing ceremony – and the haunting completely ceased.

Mr Wheaton said afterwards: 'We were dealing with the spirit of a human being who had been dead for a hundred years or more – a long-dead soldier. I severed the chains which were keeping him captive to the house where he once lived.' It was a ghostly encounter that Sheena and Emma Downs would always remember.

*   *   *   *   *

The restive ghost of an evil judge
Steeple Ashton, Wiltshire

A FEW years ago I had occasion to visit the farming village of
Steeple Ashton with its 16th-century church, its stately home,
its village green and its row of little shops. Once a prosperous weav-
ing and market town, included in the Domesday Book, it was almost
totally destroyed by fire in the early 1600s. One of the few premises
to escape the fire was a 600-year-old store run at the time of my visit
by genial Mrs Tugwood, a lady whose experiences extending over
three years had convinced her that there *are* such things as ghosts.

After spending most of their lives farming in Kent the Tugwoods
bought the village grocery store here – it had been the village court-
house in the reign of James II – and settled down to what they
hoped would be a peaceful and carefree old age.

Mrs Tugwood was rightly proud of the historic house with its massive oak beams, its heavy iron-latched doors, the thick walls of mud
and straw and the picturesque exterior – but she and her husband
had not expected a ghost and seemingly the ghost of none other
than 'Bloody' Judge Jeffreys.

The Tugwoods had scarcely moved in before they were told inde-
pendently, by several villagers, that they had a ghost upstairs, a ghost
most often seen and heard in the vicinity of an ancient, dark and
somewhat ominous cupboard.

Now Mrs Tugwood didn't believe in ghosts. As she said, she had
enough to do to cope with the problems of this world without both-
ering about the next. Of course she knew that the infamous Judge
Jeffreys had held circuit courts throughout the area into which she

86

had moved and that in Steeple Ashton they were held in the room she used as a sitting-room; the Judge seated, she was told, where her mahogany dresser now stood, sentencing men and women to be hanged on the village gallows without so much as a change of expression on his face.

It was true that both she and her husband found themselves uncharacteristically and inexplicably awake some nights, listening to the creaking that pervaded the old house and the opening of closed doors and the banging shut of open doors. There was the fact that the pigeonholed corner cupboard was often open in the morning although they both knew it had been carefully closed the night before . . . but ghosts . . .

'Then one night,' Mrs Tugwood told me, 'I was standing by the window, preparing for bed, with my husband already asleep, when loud and distinct footsteps sounded on the landing outside. As I turned towards the bedroom door I saw the iron latch lift and the door slowly open. I waited, expecting my daughter to appear but instead I saw a cloaked shadow pass from the open door to the corner cupboard and there seem to search the pigeonholes, as though seeking missing papers.

'As soon as its back was turned I dived into bed and under the clothes, too terrified even to wake my husband. But I knew what I had seen and I then knew the stories I had heard were true: we were sharing our home with a ghost.'

Mr Tugwood was sceptical but sympathetic to the experience that had befallen his wife. But a few weeks later he both heard and saw the ghost himself. He saw it so clearly that he threw his shoe at it, and the shoe sailed right through the ghost and took a chunk of plaster out of the wall – and the ghost continued ambling along towards the cupboard, completely undeterred by the presence of Mr Tugwood or anything he did.

Thereafter, I was told, the ghost was seen by both Mr and Mrs Tugwood 'frequently but irregularly'. Relatives and friends came to scoff, saw the ghost for themselves or more often heard it, and departed convinced.

There was for instance Gordon Oakes, the tough 26-year-old nephew of the Tugwoods who rushed downstairs one evening, his eyes wide and unbelieving, shouting hysterically: 'Your ghost is upstairs, Auntie; I've just seen it.'

Things became so bad that the Tugwoods knew they would have to do something about their unwelcome guest. Either they moved out, which they did not want to do; or they came to terms with the ghost, made it 'one of the family' as it were, and lived with it on friendly terms. They decided on the latter course, Mr Tugwood reasoning that the ghost appeared to have no objection to them and seemed harmless enough.

Mrs Tugwood was becoming very annoyed by the incessant opening of the bedroom door in the middle of the night, breaking her sleep and spoiling her night's rest and it was agreed that they sleep with the bedroom door open – a sort of 'Welcome Home-and-don't-wake-the-family' gesture.

'We went out of our way to make it one of the family and it never really troubled us after that,' Mrs Tugwood told me. Nevertheless she went on to say that many nights as she and her husband lay in bed they heard the 'friendly' ghost pace the landing outside the bedroom door before entering. They used to wait for it to come quietly into the room through the open door, pass the bed without seeming to notice it, and go to the corner cupboard – but by that time Mrs Tugwood told me that both she and her husband had their heads under the bedclothes!

'It's not that I'm frightened,' Mrs Tugwood told me. 'I just don't feel easy. Someone suggested I ought to speak to the ghost but I wouldn't dare . . . it might answer back!'

* * * * *

The ghostly traitor
Studland Bay, Dorset

A CORRESPONDENT tells me that he and his girlfriend had a ghostly encounter while walking on the beach opposite Studland Bay.

Anything in the nature of ghosts or paranormal activity was far from their thoughts when suddenly and at the same time they both became aware of 'a whiteish, misty figure' that seemed to be walking in unison and parallel with them along the beach, although some distance away.

They turned slantingly towards the other figure, as they sought to leave the beach but when they arrived at the point where their path and that of the 'misty figure' should have crossed, they found the beach deserted. Actually they lost sight of the form for a moment because their view was momentarily blocked by a beach hut. The form did not materialise beyond the hut and when they reached the point where they could see clearly and completely behind the hut and the whole path taken by the misty figure, not only was there no sign whatever of the figure they had been idly watching for several minutes but there seemed no possible alternative route for the figure to have taken.

My informant tells me that his girlfriend has always been psychically sensitive and often seems to have 'a perception of abstract things' and it is probably significant that throughout the whole of the walk on the beach on that particular occasion she had been feeling 'very uneasy all of the time'.

Curiously enough another correspondent has informed me of a

very similar experience on the same beach. William Sargeant and his wife (who is also occasionally psychically perceptive) had walked along the beach and back again from the beach building (which is quite close to the hut referred to in the previous experience). Neither had seen, heard or felt anything unusual during the walk or when returning and in fact the beach was deserted apart from a couple of teenagers engrossed with each other's company.

Now William and his wife were resting and enjoying a cup of tea when they both idly noticed a figure on the beach in the distance, almost in a straight line behind the hut away along the beach. The figure seemed to be too far away for them to distinguish any details but they said at the time that it looked like a man in a white suit or a girl in a white dress and there seemed to be a kind of heat haze around the figure that made it even more indistinct.

As the Sargeants chatted and drank their tea they glanced from time to time in the direction of the approaching figure. It seemed a curiously long way off and the haziness of the form made it almost appear to be floating rather than walking. After some little time it was decidedly nearer and while a haziness still clung about the figure, they both agreed that it was a man. Both found themselves referring to 'him' getting nearer.

Not wishing to appear to be consciously watching the man, who was now less than a hundred yards distant from them, the Sargeants stood up and turned away from the figure. William stooped to pick up a piece of paper that was about to blow away and in doing so noticed the man was much nearer and almost behind the nearby beach hut.

A few moments later William Sargeant and his wife, somewhat surprised that the man had not passed them, since there was nowhere else for him to go, turned together and were astonished to find the area completely deserted. They looked at one another unbelievingly and then walked towards the beach hut; William walked round to the back while his wife went round the other way. They met on the other side of the hut but of the mysterious man in white there was no sign.

Looking back on the experience they felt that his clothes could have been rather old-fashioned, a white suit and a white hat. They had no impression of his face. They were sufficiently puzzled to make some discreet enquiries locally and then they wrote to me.

They learned that there had been talk of a ghostly figure in white on that stretch of beach over the past fifty years. He was supposed to be an Englishman who worked for the Germans during the Second World War and who was finally set upon by local patriots (possibly members of the local Home Guard) and put to death somewhere on that beach. He was never seen again and his body was never found.

The ghost of a murderer
Zennor, Cornwall

I HAVE in my records firsthand evidence for some very strange happenings in a cottage on Zennor Moors.

Some months after the family moved into the large cottage not too far from Penzance they began to realise that they could not simply disregard drawings and messages that appeared mysteriously and unaccountably on the wall by the stairway. One of the curious facts (comparable with the wall writings that appeared at Borley Rectory, 'the most haunted house in England', when the paranormal activity there was at its height) is that while no one in the family was above five feet nine inches in height, none of the drawings and messages were less than five feet eleven inches high.

As the writings continued, articles in the house, and especially articles with religious associations such as a crucifix and some black beads, would be moved or would disappear completely.

Friends, staying with the family, would sometimes complain of curious sensations, such as a burning feeling in the toes. One witness said it felt just as though a lighted match had been placed under the toes but after a moment the sensation completely vanished. Several visitors reported this, none aware that the identical sensation had been experienced previously by other people. And that applied equally to the strange smells.

These smells seemed to be confined to one particular corner of one bedroom and different people described the smells differently: as resembling stale cheese, blood, sweat and human urine.

In an adjoining room, occupied by two sisters in their twenties,

'… *the son of the family awoke to find blood on his palm – the glass front of a clock was smashed, a crucifix and black beads removed …*'

voices were heard. Although no actual words were distinguishable, the tone and apparent urgency of the sounds was very frightening; as was the occasion when the son of the family awoke one night to find blood on his palm. He was unable to sleep alone in the room for several nights thereafter.

Other incidents observed or experienced by members of the family and by visitors included the smashing of the glass front of a clock and the movement of some coins (in one instance some of the missing coins were found inside the battery section of a tape recorder) and the definite but never observed movement of objects placed on one old beam in the cottage.

One seemingly impossible transportation concerned a large boiler which stood beside a door. The boiler was in fact larger than the doorway, yet it was found one morning in the adjoining room having seemingly passed through a hole too small to take its bulk!

Other disturbances included rapping sounds and voices in various parts of the cottage, some of which were recorded on tape; and an indistinct figure was seen standing in the kitchen doorway.

Curiously enough a few months after receiving one report on this case I received another, from an entirely different source but reporting very similar activity in the same area. Here some form of contact seems to have been made with the ill-defined figure that lingered in a doorway and it was established to the satisfaction of the people concerned that a former resident had been responsible for the death of someone in the 'haunted' bedroom and was seeking to draw attention to the fact in the hope of obtaining peace.

After considerable research and patient and sympathetic involvement with the entity, the disturbances abated and when I last heard from this family they had experienced nothing untoward for several weeks and were holding their breath in the hope that their sympathetic understanding and sincere wish to help the haunting entity had in fact freed the unhappy haunter from any necessity for further encounters with the present occupant of the Cornish cottage.

By the same author ...

Ghosts of Cornwall
Ghosts of Devon
Ghosts of Somerset
Ghosts of Dorset
Ghosts of Wiltshire
Westcountry Hauntings
Mysterious Places
The Ghost Hunter's Guide
This Haunted Isle
Queen Victoria's Other World
Dictionary of the Supernatural
The Ghost Hunters
Haunted London
Into the Occult
Deeper Into the Occult
Gazetteer of British Ghosts
Gazetteer of Scottish and Irish Ghosts
Ghosts of Wales
Hauntings: New Light on Ten Famous Cases
A Host of Hauntings
The Vampire's Bedside Companion
The Complete Book of Dowsing and Divining
Ghosts of North West England
Ghosts of Kent
A Ghost Hunter's Handbook
Ghosts of Hampshire and the Isle of Wight
Lives to Remember: A Casebook on Reincarnation
        (with Leonard Wilder)
The Ghosts of Borley: A critical history of the
        'most haunted house in England' (with Dr Paul Tabori)
Jack the Ripper: One Hundred Years of Mystery
Death in Hollywood

Biography
Horror Man – The Life of Boris Karloff
Life's a Drag – A Life of Danny la Rue

As Editor
Thirteen Famous Ghost Stories (Everyman's Library)

MORE BOSSINEY BOOKS ...

PARANORMAL IN THE WESTCOUNTRY
by Michael Williams

SUPERNATURAL IN SOMERSET
by Rosemary Clinch

MYSTERIES IN THE CORNISH LANDSCAPE
by Tamsin Thomas

SOMERSET MYSTERIES
by Polly Lloyd & Michael Williams

WILTSHIRE MYSTERIES
Introduced by David Foot

CURIOSITIES OF EXMOOR
by Felicity Young

We shall be pleased to send you our catalogue giving full details of our growing list of titles for Cornwall, Devon, Dorset, Somerset, Avon and Wiltshire. If you have difficulty in obtaining our titles, write direct to Bossiney Books, Land's End, St Teath, Bodmin, Cornwall.